LIFE
The American Immigrant

LIFE

Editor Robert Sullivan
Creative Director Ian Denning
Picture Editor Barbara Baker Burrows
Executive Editor Robert Andreas
Art Director Lynda D'Amico
Associate Picture Editor Christina Lieberman
Writer-Reporters Hildegard Anderson (Chief),
Lindsey Lee Johnson
Copy JC Choi (Chief), Mimi McGrath, Wendy Williams
Production Manager Michael Roseman
Picture Research Rachel Hendrick
Photo Assistant Joshua Colow
Consulting Picture Editors
Suzanne Hodgart (London), Tala Skari (Paris)

Publisher Andrew Blau
Finance Director Craig Ettinger
Assistant Finance Manager Karen Tortora

Editorial Operations Richard K. Prue (Director),
Richard Shaffer (Manager), Brian Fellows, Raphael Joa,
Stanley E. Moyse (Supervisors), Keith Aurelio, Gregg Baker,
Charlotte Coco, Scott Dvorin, Kevin Hart, Rosalie Khan,
Po Fung Ng, Barry Pribula, David Spatz, Vaune Trachtman,
Sara Wasilausky, David Weiner

Time Inc. Home Entertainment

President Rob Gursha
Vice President, New Product Development Richard Fraiman
Executive Director, Marketing Services Carol Pittard
Director, Retail & Special Sales Tom Mifsud
Director of Finance Tricia Griffin
Assistant Marketing Director Ann Marie Doherty
Prepress Manager Emily Rabin
Book Production Manager Jonathan Polsky
Associate Product Manager Jennifer Dowell

Special thanks to Bozena Bannett, Alexandra Bliss,
Bernadette Corbie, Robert Dente, Gina Di Meglio,
Anne-Michelle Gallero, Peter Harper, Suzanne Janso,
Robert Marasco, Natalie McCrea, Margarita Quiogue,
Mary Jane Rigoroso, Steven Sandonato, Grace Sullivan

Published by

LIFE Books

"LIFE" is a trademark of
Time Inc.

Time Inc.
1271 Avenue of the Americas,
New York, NY 10020

We welcome your comments
and suggestions about LIFE
Books. Please write to us at:
LIFE Books, Attention:
Book Editors, PO Box 11016,
Des Moines, IA 50336-1016

If you would like to order any
of our hardcover Collector's
Edition books, please call us
at 1-800-327-6388 (Monday
through Friday, 7:00 a.m.–
8:00 p.m. or Saturday, 7:00
a.m.–6:00 p.m. Central Time).

ISBN: 1-932273-63-8
Library of Congress Control
Number: 2004108512

Please visit us, and sample
past editions of LIFE, at
www.LIFE.com.

Classic images from the pages and covers of LIFE are now
available. Posters can be ordered at www.LIFEposters.com. Fine
art prints from the LIFE Picture Collection and the LIFE Gallery
of Photography can be viewed at www.LIFEphotographs.com.

Irving Berlin, in 1943's *Show Business at War*

Into America

FOREWORD BY Frank McCourt

We knew who discovered America: St. Brendan the Navigator. It's not something the Italians like to hear—not to mention the Vikings—but Irish history is Irish history and different from all other histories.

We knew who built America: the Irish. It was all up there on the screen at the Lyric Cinema in Limerick, Ireland. It's not something other ethnic groups like to hear about but there was no getting around the names that built railroads and canals and ran the great political machines in the big cities. Irish.

There was little to be proud of at home—eight hundred years of subjugation and lamentation—but, boy, did we make up for it when we arrived in America!

If I know anything about American history I learned it by going through that Irish door. I had read textbooks on American history and taken courses but they were dull, dull, dull. Not a bit like Irish history, where something was always happening, always a fight or a promise of a fight and would you like to step outside?

When I taught at various high schools around New York I heard the students complain about their American history classes and I didn't understand. The movies at the Lyric Cinema opened up to us an American past that was glorious, colorful and sweeping, and with music playing no matter what happened. One of my earliest memories is of a movie with Deborah Kerr in which she plays the

wife of William Penn, how he came to America with a vision of peace and love. There were the westerns, classic in form and subject: the lone gunman; noble Indian chiefs; forts attacked, scalps taken; gunfighter showdowns on Main Street; whiskey knocked back by the bottleful; chaste blond heroines and dark-haired temptresses; the hero in white, the bad guy in black.

Then there were the gangster movies with our Cuchulain, James Cagney, up to all kinds of devilment, and Father Pat O'Brien praying over him. And how about Hopalong Cassidy? What does his name suggest?

There were peripheral Italians, Greeks, Germans but they were included in films only for comedy or

The myth (and sometimes the reality) of the American immigrant's story, as told by Hollywood: Deborah Kerr and Clifford Evans in *Penn of Pennsylvania*; Charlie Chaplin and Edna Purviance in *The Immigrant*.

Everett Collection

Pat O'Brien prays for James Cagney, who is on his way to "the chair" in *Angels with Dirty Faces.* **Opposite: Director Elia Kazan based his epic immigration tale,** *America, America,* **on the experience of his Greek uncle, who fled Turkey. Here, in steerage, desperate Europeans dream of America.**

cooking. It was the Irish who nobly went toe to toe with everyone, killed the Indians, fought on both sides in the Civil War, joined the cops, fought the Mafia, earned the most medals of honor of any ethnic group—or so we were told.

American history sneaks up on you. It can come in shapes of huddled masses, barrows in streets, cries of hawkers, whores in Victorian doorways, lines of doomed infantrymen moving toward one another at Gettysburg, Roosevelt soothing our Great Depression fears or telling the Daughters of the American Revolution we are all immigrants.

The Lower East Side of Manhattan is a great multilayered museum of American immigration. Walk the streets. Look at the old tenements with fire escapes where families slept during sizzling summers. Sigh over bricked-up synagogues. Imagine the people moving through these streets between the Civil War and World War II: the Irish, Germans, Jews, Italians. Closer to our time came the Chinese and Puerto Ricans. The walls tell stories. The streets sing of romances on stoops, stickball, men going to war, returning as heroes or maimed or not at all.

Take the ferry to Ellis Island and prepare to

weep. This is the Golden Door and yet a tragic place. You'll see in the Great Hall a mound of bags, trunks, boxes. In other rooms are glass cases filled with the artifacts of exile: books, clothes, rosary beads, babies' shoes, diaries. You might find yourself holding your breath. These are your people—it does not matter where you come from.

This is where I forget I'm Irish, where I don't care. I'm with that Albanian man, his wife, and his two children with their great dark eyes. I'm with that Russian woman having her eyelids rolled back by a trachoma hunter. "Sorry, ma'am. You can't enter America with those eyes." Or, "Sorry, you have tuberculosis."

Jesus. How did they survive it, the ones who were turned away? To have traveled across Europe and Atlantic, betrayed at the Door by eyes or lungs or an uncomprehending mind? To be escorted along Manhattan piers and put aboard another ship while their families wailed on the docks? Is there a single story or novel or play about the terrible tragedy of the rejects? And their families? Maybe some were smart enough, eventually, to sneak in through Canada.

But the East Coast is only part of it. We know the Chinese struggle, how they worked on the Central Pacific Railroad, how they brought supplies to the wild men in the '49 Gold Rush, how they did the laundry and cooked and prospered in San Francisco till a mad Irishman, Denis Kearney, ranted and waved signs that said, CHINESE MUST GO.

They were excluded for a time but they hung on, and you can't imagine San Francisco or New York or a dozen other cities without them.

Every ethnic group has a story. They get into this country one way or another. They dig in, work like ants, beavers—the animal of your choice. They wear themselves out but they insist on education for their children—and that's the main story. You could travel from graduation to graduation around this country and you'd find parents in the audience barely understanding the speeches that say "Go forth." The parents wouldn't understand that clichéd admonition one bit. "What's this 'Go forth?' Do you have to be told this, Son, Daughter, by some speechifying politician?"

In the old westerns I watched at the Lyric Cinema, I squirmed with pleasure when the wagon master called "Move out," and whips cracked and men urged on horses and oxen and women and children gazed out of the wagons and music soared from a heavenly orchestra and you knew that out there lay all kinds of danger—locusts, outlaws, drought, Apaches, impassable mountains, no, never impassable, not if they had to lift the damn wagons over the peaks and if they kept on, they'd come to lush lands where they could claim hundreds of acres and live a good fresh sinewy life.

Oh, man, it was almost too much for me up in the balcony, all that land and sky and greatness of heart and vision, those tremendous people in their Conestoga wagons, good-humored, unblinking, ready for anything. Native or foreign-born, they rode from horizon to horizon and that, for me, is the American story.

Frank McCourt, author of Angela's Ashes, *about his youth in Ireland, and* 'Tis, *which is set in America, taught for 30 years in New York City public schools.*

The First Americans

By Choice, By Accident, By Force

Before the huddled masses, intrepid individuals came in search of adventure, freedom or simply a new start. They were pioneers. They were immigrants.

Some historians see the first great wave of U.S. immigration as the one beginning in the early 19th century when, for political or personal reasons, hundreds of thousands of Europeans made their way to America's shores. But the ebb and flow of the American immigration story began much, much earlier. You have to go back some 20,000 years to locate this country's first immigrants, Asians who made their way across the Bering land bridge, then migrated south and became over time what we now know as the Native Americans. And much later came Vikings, conquistadors, settlers, slaves—in a whole series of different and fascinating episodes of immigration, both voluntary and otherwise.

During the last Ice Age, oceans receded when glaciers stole their water. Slowly, Asia, which was already populated by man, and North America—which was not—became a single landmass, Beringia, as terra firma emerged in the northern seas. The "bridge" was in actuality a vast plain of tundra 1,000 miles wide, linking what is now Alaska to what is now Siberia. Beringia was twice the size of Texas, and new evidence shows that melting ice and rising seas didn't sink this bridge until perhaps as recently as 11,000 years ago. At that point, Asian nomads and their descendants who were in North America saw the door close behind them. To put it in a more positive light, they were bequeathed a new world to shape as they saw fit.

Today, the shortest open-water expanse between Alaska and Siberia is the Bering Strait, 55 miles across. Midway lie two land-bridge remnants, the Diomede Islands. In days of yore, nearly all the water in this photo was land.

In the North American West—and eventually the East—they were citizens of multitudinous tribes of "Indians." In Central and South America they built the glorious Mayan, Incan and Aztec civilizations. For a hundred centuries, they had the land to themselves.

Leif Eriksson was an Icelandic Viking who, the saga goes, followed up on rumors of an Eden to the west, and became the first European to land in America—about 1,000 years ago. Neither he nor his men had any interest in immigrating, though 160 Greenlanders who followed in their wake did. Hostile terrain and Indians were dissuasive, and this early attempt at colonization failed in three years' time. Another 500 years would pass before Native Americans would again be accosted by foreigners.

In 1492, Christopher Columbus, an Italian admiral in the employ of Spain, sailed with a diverse crew—Irish, English, Jewish and black were present—aboard three ships from Palos to the Bahamas. (As with Eriksson, he had hoped to land elsewhere—in Columbus's case, Cathay, or China.) He and other European adventurers made round-trip voyages in the years that followed, prospecting, settling, cultivating friends and enemies, changing the land and the culture forevermore. They reached the North American mainland, and introduced to the millions of natives living there such exotica as the pig and the horse, new strains of grain and fruit, new ideas of government and religion, all manner of new disease to which the Indians had no immunities and to which they succumbed in astonishing

The uninvited: When Columbus traveled to the West Indies (far left), he enslaved the natives there. Cortés (left) sacked the Aztec empire. Ponce de León (below) Christianized many Florida natives against their will. De Soto went west from his 1539 Florida bivouac (opposite) to defeat Indians en route to discovering the Mississippi River.

An English armada returns to Roanoke in 1590, expecting to resupply the colony. Instead, they would find the colony gone—vanished entirely—and to this day, the fate of those settlers remains unknown.

numbers. The genocide later visited upon Native Americans when Manifest Destiny drew the white man westward was mild compared with the diseases introduced by the first Europeans between 1500 and 1600 that killed perhaps 90 percent of all North American Indians.

The Spanish conquistadors—Cortés, Pizarro—and the mercenary gold seekers of the 1500s hardly qualify as immigrants, but many who traveled into America with explorers including Balboa, de Soto, Ponce de León and Coronado chose to stay, sometimes intermarrying with the natives, and can be seen as pioneers of the melting pot. Spanish missions and forts rose in the Deep South and Far West, while in the East, territories were claimed for France and England by Jacques Cartier and John Cabot (who was actually an Italian, Giovanni Caboto, working for King Henry VII). The English in particular made organized efforts to establish colonies. Emigrating from there beginning in 1585 were scores of men and women responding to the charge that Queen Elizabeth had given Sir Walter Raleigh: "[T]o discover barbarous countries, not actually possessed of any Christian prince and inhabited by Christian people, to occupy and enjoy the same for ever." The future was short indeed for the first groups who tried to settle Roanoke Island off what is now North Carolina. The 1585 contingent per-

suaded Sir Francis Drake to return them home from this godforsaken place, and the 1587 group of 91 men, 17 women and 9 children are immortal still as the Lost Colony—they went missing altogether, leaving behind only an inscrutable name carved in a tree. More successful by several degrees was the 1607 settlement at Jamestown in Virginia, which saw 46 of its 104 original members die within four months but which, through the generosity of local natives who shared corn and fish, persevered through the first winter, and then through the "starving time" winter of 1609-1610, when Jamestown's replenished population was reduced from about 500 to 60. Jamestown was and is the first permanent English settlement in America.

Another famous early English settlement was farther to the north. In 1620 a group of Puritans, seeking freedom to worship as they chose, fled England and made landfall near what is now called Plymouth Rock in Massachusetts. As with the Jamestownians, they received assistance from benevolent Indians—and were lucky for it. The first year was brutal, but the Pilgrims survived. Grace notes were shared during the 1621 harvest when natives and immigrants broke bread together in a three-day celebration. Some two and a half centuries later, the event would be commemorated when President Abraham Lincoln called for a

national day of thanksgiving.

The 17th century, taken as a whole, can be seen as a blueprint for the American immigration story; all the dynamics, tensions, triumphs and troubles that would attend future assimilations were present from the get-go. Most of those who would come to America were refugees from something, often war or religious persecution, or were being transported to do dirty work for the colonials. (Some 50,000 convicts and debtors were among the earliest English settlers, and later, the tough-as-nails Scotch-Irish were recruited to push into the Appalachian wilderness, a place full of "savages" and savage beasts.) Where there had been trouble at home, there was often trouble abroad. War and poor harvest in England caused 20,000 to emigrate to New England between 1630 and 1643—theirs was called the Great Migration—but not all found what they were looking for. The Puritans of the newly formed Massachusetts Bay Colony, now with

Africans began to be captured and forced into bondage as early as the 1440s, when the Portuguese started selling them in Europe. The complicity of West African rulers in the enterprise remains an open wound.

the upper hand, were intolerant of the refugee Baptists, Quakers and Presbyterians, even though they themselves had similarly been persecuted in England. Members of the unwanted sects moved on to other parts of New England and, subsequently, to Pennsylvania. A pattern quickly took shape among the white settlers: Last year's immigrants, climbing the ladder, made sure that this year's immigrants started at the bottom.

Four years after the Pilgrims landed in Plymouth, the first Dutch immigrants landed on Manhattan Island. Two years later they bought it from the natives in a deal that would make Donald Trump shiver with pride, and even as they built Nieuw Amsterdam, they pushed farther up the Hudson River, establishing villages along the way. All seafaring nations were now in the game. In 1637, Dutch, German and Swedish entrepreneurs formed the New Sweden Company, a trading firm, and Scandinavian settlements eventually dominated the Delaware River Valley. The Portuguese came. The Danes. The French. In 1664 the British conquered Nieuw Amsterdam and found themselves in charge of a populace speaking in 18 different languages

including Czech and Polish—a toddling version of today's New York City.

French fur trappers in the North and farmers in the Deep South . . . Italian glassmakers and German craftsmen in the Northeast . . . Mennonites, Moravians, Calvinists, Lutherans, Pietists, Quakers, Jews and Dunkers on the run . . . they all came to America. They came, for the most part, of their own accord, and for reasons that would echo down through history. However, there was one development in the 17th and early 18th century that was a different matter entirely.

African slaves had been brought into Jamestown very shortly after the settlement's founding, and therefore the institution of slavery in America dates quite nearly to the white man's appearance on these shores. This chapter is often omitted in histories of immigration because, after all, the West Africans might technically have immigrated, but they were hardly emigrants—not in the sense that they bade their homeland goodbye to find a future elsewhere. They were kidnapped, plain and simple, most often by other Africans seeking the white man's blood money. They were then sold into an industry so bru-

The "cargo" was wedged between decks. "The slaves were all enclosed under grated hatchways," ran one contemporaneous account. "The space was so low that they sat between each other's legs and [were] stowed so close together that there was no possibility of their lying down or changing their position . . . The heat of these horrid places was so great and the odor so offensive . . ." By some estimates, one of every five slaves died during the passage from Africa.

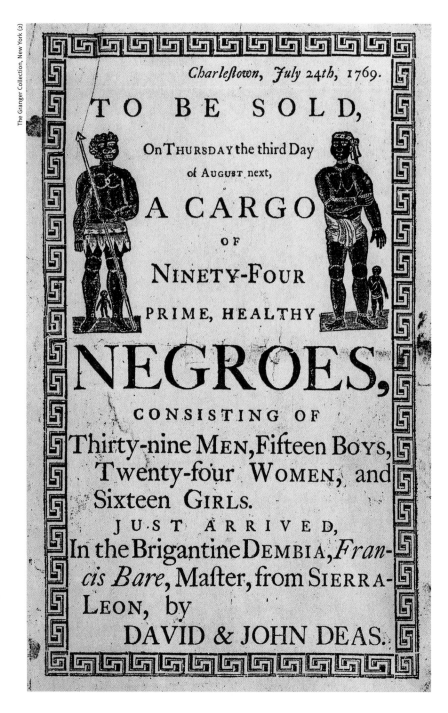

This 1769 broadside advertises a shipment of slaves for sale by the brothers Deas, South Carolina slave-traders. The state had a long history of slavery already, having forced Native Americans into bondage since early in the 17th century.

tal and morally bereft as to defy comprehension. The Africans were tools or commodities to their owners—animals, at best.

Today, blacks represent a sixth of the U.S. population; descendants of slaves number some 38 million. In fact, very shortly after the founding of the country—in 1790, when the first census was taken—the largest group of non–Native Americans in the 13 states was of English heritage, numbering about 1.9 million, but the second largest, at 757,208, was African American. That total was greater than the combined Scotch and Irish populations, and larger than the German, Dutch, French, Swedish—all others—combined.

Looked at another way, it's a small figure. From about 1450 to 1870, some 10 million Africans were captured, the vast majority of them destined for the Americas. But only about 400,000 were sent to what is now the U.S., with the rest going to the Caribbean islands, as well as South and Central America. Nowhere, however, would the presence of slaves—the *fact* of slaves and the concept of slaveholding—have such an impact on the national consciousness as it did in "the land of the free."

Even as the nation was forming and its intentions were being put on paper, observers commented on the promise of liberty in this New World enterprise. The French-born J. Hector St. John Crèvecoeur, whose influential *Letters from an American Farmer* was published in 1782, expressed the ideal succinctly: "There is room for everybody in America." But not for slaves, some of whom were held even by certain Founding Fathers, notably Thomas Jefferson, who kept 187 on his Virginia estate, never freeing them during his lifetime. The inconsistency of slavery with America's notions of democracy was clear from the first; it is apparent from Jefferson's writings that even some slaveholders grappled with the question. Yet it would take a Civil War, and then many subsequent generations of social evolution, to approach anything like equal rights. Even today, racial equality remains a central issue in the United States.

Unfortunately, as abominable as the African experience in early America was, that of the people who once dominated this land—the Native Americans—was its equal. The earliest European-Indian encounters presaged those to come: Some were peaceful, many others were violent. Consid-

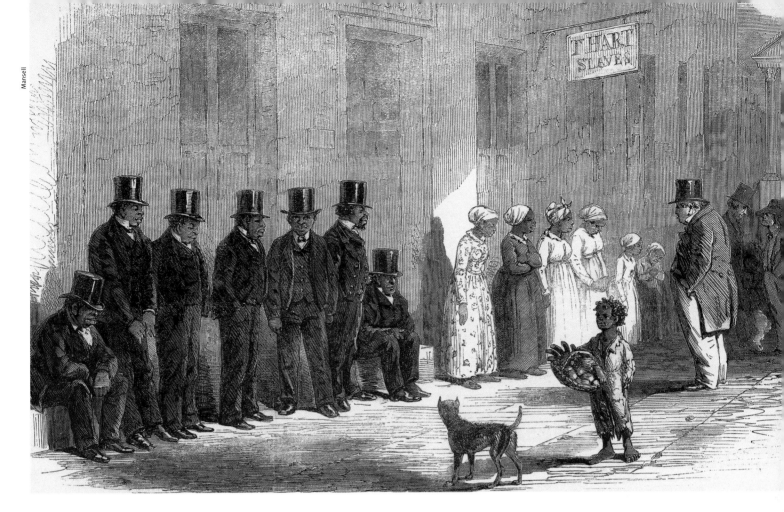

er the Pocahontas story. What is remembered is that she saved the Englishman John Smith from death at the hands of her people, the Powhatans, then later married John Rolfe to secure a peace between the Indians and the immigrants. But surrounding details indicate just what a tinderbox Jamestown was. In 1607, the year Smith was captured and brought before Wahunsonacock, conflicts were constant between settlers and the Powhatans. In 1613, the year before she married Rolfe, Pocahontas herself was captured by the British Captain Argall and held as ransom for Englishmen who were prisoners of the tribe. And in 1622, six years after Rolfe and Pocahontas departed for England, the Powhatans attacked Jamestown, killing 350 while suffering massive losses themselves when the settlers fought back ferociously.

That the Dutch bought 15,000 acres of Manhattan in 1626 for trinkets worth 60 guilders—not quite $30 today—seems a quaint, almost decorous East Coast swindle when compared with the fate of western Indians who were made to work as slaves in immigrant mining operations. To be sure, the Native Americans, when they were able to discern what was happening, fought back—but fate

Families were split up, children wrenched from parents—the individuals sold for respective strengths or talents. In New Orleans, slaves are dressed for domestic duties and put on display. In 1741 in Nieuw Amsterdam, the city fathers blamed several fires on an unproved slave revolt. After a rush to judgment, 17 blacks were hanged and 13 burned at the stake.

The conqueror sometimes paid for his sins: Spaniards exploit slaves in their 16th century mining efforts, then one of them is made to swallow molten gold. Left: Minuit buys Manhattan. According to one account, the Indians saw the transaction as but a gesture, since they had no concept of "ownership."

was not on their side.

One man's life is emblematic. The Shawnee Tecumseh was born in 1768 in Ohio and raised to be a warrior. In the late 18th century, Scotch-Irish settlers, supported by the Army, were pushing the boundaries of their country over the Appalachians and into the Midwest. Tecumseh was yet a boy when he fought in his first battle against the Army in 1782, but became a leader by 1791 when he was victorious against Arthur St. Clair's men in the Northwest Territory.

Tecumseh knew the white man would keep coming, and felt the Indians' best hope was to unite and make a stand west of the Appalachians. He traveled from Canada to the Gulf of Mexico coaxing many different tribes to form a confederation. In 1808 he and his brother, the Prophet, established Prophetstown in the Indiana Territory—a de facto capital of the rising Indian nation. The territorial governor William Henry Harrison didn't like what he saw, and in 1811 he marched toward Prophetstown. He won an overwhelming victory at the Battle of Tippecanoe, then destroyed the Indians' village. Tecumseh had been away on yet another diplomatic mission, and returned to devastation. Events intervened in the form of the War of 1812. Tecumseh allied with the British in hopes that, should they prevail, they might give back to the Indians their homelands. Tecumseh was killed by Harrison's men at the Battle of the Thames in 1813, and with him died not only the dream of an Indian nation but, in fact, whatever hope the Indians had in the face of the white man's advance.

This was the country, then, early in the 19th century: a place of equality and inequality, idealism and barbarity, hope and despair—and unparalleled potential. From afar, with the news filtered by distance, it looked like a land of opportunity, a welcoming shore in desperate times.

A tidal wave was about to crash.

Tecumseh thought an Indian nation might live in peace alongside the United States. Then he hoped the enemy of the United States might be his friend, and he threw in with the British. Finally, he was killed.

The Field Museum

The Promised Land

1815–1860

The docks of Liverpool were the way station for hundreds of thousands who sought America. Some, particularly the poor Irish, got this far but didn't have the money to continue on, and so their immigration story ended in England, Scotland or Wales.

As the Napoleonic Wars finally drew to a close in Europe in 1815, a new wave of immigration was forming, one in which five million people would make their way to America. The promise of this new world now cast a beacon to many different lands, and, interestingly, for the multitudes who were drawn by its warming brilliance, this light contained very different hues. Of course, while each individual summons his own reason for leaving his native land, there were common motivations, and consequences, for those who now came. These emigrants, from wherever they hailed, tended to leave their given country for the same sorts of reasons, and once in America, these ex-countrymen often had a shared experience and altered their new home in singular, defining ways.

To wit, the Irish. Their British rulers had left them almost entirely reliant on a single tuber for sustenance. In the past, the potato had suffered many blights, but in 1845, *Phytophthora infestans* struck like a plague, and famine, with its familiar henchmen disease and misery, drove the Irish from their land. More than a million of these refugees came to America, and usually they came with tattered clothes and empty pockets. Their sea voyages, often made in "coffin ships," were little better than the passage endured by slaves. Once on these shores, they found no warm embrace but rather thieves, or "runners" who lured them to scurrilous landlords. And worse.

As John F. Kennedy stated in his book *A Nation of Immigrants,* "The Irish were the first to endure the scorn and discrimination later to be inflicted, to some degree at least, on each successive wave of immigrants by already settled 'Americans.'" The future President noted, "They were mostly country folk, small farmers, cottagers and farm laborers. Yet they congregated mainly in cities along the Eastern seaboard, for they did not have the money to travel after reaching shore. Few could read or write; some spoke only Gaelic." Discrimination, often of a religious nature, made desirable work hard to find—NO IRISH NEED APPLY—and so most took positions as domestics or laborers.

By settling in the cities, the Irish would gradually find their way into the law, and then government. They would create exceptional universities, even as they changed the Catholic Church in America from a French institution to an English-speaking one. They would truly carve a niche into what had essentially been a homogeneous nation. And in so doing, as Kennedy wrote, they "eased the way for other immigrant groups . . . The schools they founded offered educational opportunities to children of later immigrants of other tongues . . . Workers of Irish descent helped organize . . . the forerunner of the American Federation of Labor."

Shortly after the Irish, Germans began to arrive in great numbers. For some, following the failure of the 1848 Revolution, the old ways were no longer endurable. In a diary written in 1848 by Michael Friedrich Radke, a clear portrait is drawn of conditions in Germany for the less well-to-do: "If one appears before a court of law, or an official, or a police officer, he must always appear in a bent position and with a bent head."

Aside from the social rebels, the majority of Germans were reacting to economic conditions. Unlike the Irish, they arrived in the U.S. with some resources, which allowed them to move past the cities to the cheap, available farmlands, where their scientific approach to crops and soil conservation let them prosper. Those who remained in the city would have an important impact on such industries as steel, food, brewing and printing.

The Germans had another salient effect on the American society, as Kennedy pointed out—"the mellowing of the austere Puritan imprint on our daily lives. The Puritans observed the Sabbath as a day of silence and solemnity. The Germans clung to their concept of the 'Continental Sunday' as a day, not only of churchgoing, but also of relaxation, of picnics, of visiting, of quiet drinking in beer gardens while listening to the music of a band." Thus is a culture shaped.

Britons continued to cross, but it was these Irish and Germans who made up about two thirds of this second wave. Another part of Europe, Scandinavia, became a larger factor than theretofore. By 1860, some 125,000 Swedes, Norwegians and Danes sought out the United States. Many of them were small farmers who were finding good land scarcer and scarcer; others came in search of greater religious tolerance than was possible in their primarily Lutheran nations.

So Northern Europe was responsible for the lion's share of these new Americans, but there was also an influx from the other side of the world.

Word of the California gold rush reached Hong Kong in 1849, and thousands of Chinese, lashed by civil discord and poverty, decided to venture to the land they would call Gold Mountain. Many arrived as laborers who had traded their promise of work for the price of the ocean passage. Once in California, they became a counterpart to the Irish on the East Coast, forced to find whatever jobs they could, usually as menials, perhaps doing "women's work," cooking and washing.

Five million new Americans. This number may not seem so vast today, but it surpassed the entire population of the country as recently as 1790. The impact of the newcomers on this young land was irresistible, and immeasurable.

In this painting from 1854, an Irishman studies the daunting fares for passage to the dream that is New York City. Since 1844, nearly two million Irish, about a quarter of the country's entire population, had emigrated to the United States. Nearly half that number died during the Great Famine.

Photo12/Polaris

Above: In 1846, the year after the first potato harvest failed, families in the west of Ireland go to the seashore to collect limpets and seaweed for food. Right: a peasant's hut.

The Granger Collection, New York (2)

In 1846, a total of 92,484 Irish fled to the United States; in 1847 another 196,224; in 1848 another 173,744; 204,771 in 1849; 206,041 the following year . . . Between 1846 and 1851, the year that this illustration of emigrants on the quay at Cobh (Cork) appeared in the *London Illustrated News,* 2,227 ships completed 2,743 voyages across the Atlantic and delivered 652,931 Irish immigrants to New York City alone. The majority of them went via Liverpool.

Culver Pictures

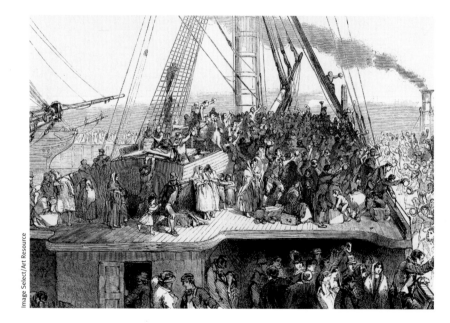

Image Select/Art Resource

Brown Brothers

Irish emigrants who were headed for North America or havens as far as Australia usually made a first stop in London or Liverpool. Above: At Prince's Landing, passengers board seagoing steamers. Left: leaving Liverpool for America in 1850. Right: A photo taken later shows the port still bustling. Liverpool would not know a frenzy like the 1840s, or send a more eager group to New York, until the Beatles led the British Invasion of 1964.

The *Ocean Monarch* departed Liverpool for America on August 24, 1848, with 396 aboard. As we see in this lithograph made soon after, it was an ill-starred journey. Six miles off North Wales, a fire spread out of control. Although nearby vessels came to her aid, the *Monarch* went down and 178 lives were lost. These ocean voyages were often perilous. Crowded, unsanitary conditions created an ideal environment for the spreading of disease. If weather conditions roughened, passengers might have to help man the ship, even though they had never been at sea before. By 1854, matters had improved, but still, it has been estimated that one out of six emigrants became seriously ill or died. But as English weaver John Downe wrote to his wife, "I would rather cross the Atlantic ten times than hear my children cry for victuals once."

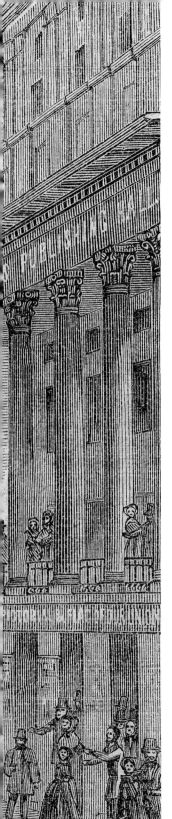

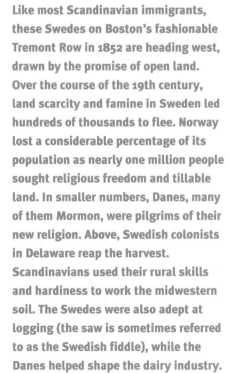

Like most Scandinavian immigrants, these Swedes on Boston's fashionable Tremont Row in 1852 are heading west, drawn by the promise of open land. Over the course of the 19th century, land scarcity and famine in Sweden led hundreds of thousands to flee. Norway lost a considerable percentage of its population as nearly one million people sought religious freedom and tillable land. In smaller numbers, Danes, many of them Mormon, were pilgrims of their new religion. Above, Swedish colonists in Delaware reap the harvest. Scandinavians used their rural skills and hardiness to work the midwestern soil. The Swedes were also adept at logging (the saw is sometimes referred to as the Swedish fiddle), while the Danes helped shape the dairy industry.

Arriving in New York Harbor en route to Castle Garden, the nation's first official immigrant processing center. When it opened in 1855, it was a welcome haven from the harrowing dock scenes of the past. By the time of its closing in 1890, however, it was overcrowded and rife with abuse. Right: Charles Frederic Ulrich titled his oil painting *In the Land of Promise.*

Completed as a military
fort in 1811, Castle Garden
(as it was later called)
would serve as an opera
house, an immigration
center—eight million
people passed through its
doors—an aquarium and,
today, a visitors' center.

In 1848 it was a frontier town with barely a thousand people. A year and a half later, gold rush fever had made San Francisco 100 times bigger. At left and below, "49ers" display their mining gear and gather with curious townsfolk in northern California's American River Basin to exchange news and gossip. Opposite, Chinese miners pan for fortune in the California soil.

Market Square in Germantown, Pa., sets a bucolic scene. During this period, many such towns cropped up in what would be known as the "German triangle," the area including St. Louis, Cincinnati and Milwaukee. Opposite: German John Jacob Astor arrived in the U.S. at age 21, penniless. But he was possessed of a remarkable business savvy; he once advised, "You should buy Manhatten [sic]—they aren't making anymore of it." He was right about that, and much else. With furs and real estate, he built an immense fortune, and at the time of his death in 1848 at age 85, he was worth $20 million (about $78 billion today)—an immigrant, and also the richest man in America.

All-American Food

Yes, all politics is local, and all cuisine is ethnic. To deconstruct the most basic plate at the Great American Cookout: The chips derive from a French potato treatment imported from Paris by none other than Thomas Jefferson; the hot dog descends from Germans who liked their wieners *mit kraut* (though sausages are referenced in Homer's *Odyssey*); and the corn—well, its relative, maize—predates the first Thanksgiving as part of a Native American's native American diet. Leif Eriksson left no strong tradition of Scandinavian cooking, but as early as Columbus, Mediterranean flavors and aromas were infiltrating the New World. The staples of other lands became, over time, all-American: Italy's pizza, France's clam chowder, even China's egg roll, wholly appropriated as the star of the puu-puu platter (tough to find in Beijing).

Doughnuts? Heisted from Holland.

If America, by dint of its multicultural society, reinvented many dishes, it has taken a while to develop a reputation for refining or advancing them. And yet, after decades of dwelling in the culinary cellar—along with the likes of the Irish and the Brits—in recent years the idea of "American cuisine," with its fusions and latter-day intoxication with freshness, has become the real deal, as have the country's many delectable wines and beers. Metaphor imitating life: An ultimate representation of the power of the melting pot is to be found in . . . the melting pot.

RED
PEPPER

Get your red hots! Or, if you're this woman, get your pizza. Or, if you're these fellows in New York City in 1960, get your kosher Chinese at Bernstein's on Chinese Night. Or, if you're these two, get your fries at Snead's in Belton, Mo. Now, back to hot dogs: Americans eat seven billion each summer, enough to stretch to the moon nearly seven times.

John Anthony Rizzo/Brand X

Bettmann/Corbis

Ed Lallo

During New York City's Feast of San Gennaro, the air is spiced with the aroma of grilled sausage. Across the country at Dodger Stadium, a hawker pushes . . . no, not peanuts or Cracker Jack but fresh sushi. During a break on the set of *The Crowd* in 1928, James Murray attacks a doughnut in a way that might appear foreign to the Dutch. Costar Eleanor Boardman does better with her cup of tea.

Growing Pains

1861–1920

Having emerged from the intense, formal scrutiny that greeted immigrants upon their arrival in the United States, this family stands on the dock at New York's Ellis Island, awaiting the government ferry that will transport them to their land of dreams.

With the advent of the 1860s, the United States would endure one of its greatest trials, the Civil War. In the course of this terrible struggle, large numbers of the newest Americans would play important roles. While many fought on the Confederate side, whole regiments composed almost entirely of one ethnicity—mainly Irish or German—were prominent fighting units for the Union.

Some of the Germans, in fact, had come specifically to fight for the North and in turn receive a land bounty when their hitch was up. That was a reward offered to the aspiring class, but it should also be recalled that America was already in the business of protecting its elite. Under the rules of the 1863 Conscription Act, the wealthy could buy their way out of the draft for $300, which was about half the annual wage of the working class.

This fact, coupled with the possible ramifications of a Union victory, led to one of the most shameful episodes in the history of the Irish American immigrant. Whereas New Yorkers had generally been proud to volunteer in 1861, when the city began enforcing the new draft act, laborers, anxious that slave emancipation would result in postwar competition for their jobs, grew incensed over the inequity inherent in the law. On July 13, 1863, two days after the first draft lottery was held in the city, an Irish mob began four days of rioting that saw police, a recruitment center and several black neighborhoods attacked. The Colored Orphan Asylum was burned; the Aged Colored Woman's Home was also torched. More than 100 died before Union troops, including veterans of Gettysburg, put down the violence. The Draft Riots inflamed anti-Irish sentiment in the North—even as many first- and second-generation immigrants from the Emerald Isle were fighting for the cause.

Another piece of legislation that made a huge impact on immigrants and would-be immigrants was also hatched during the war. With the Homestead Act of 1862, Congress decreed that any adult citizen, or any alien who intended to become a citizen, could get title to 160 acres by working the land for five years (or by paying $1.25 an acre). A lot of folks took advantage of the offer, and profited from it. Although an outsize portion of the public land ended up in the hands of speculators and the railroads, the Homestead Act did help send a half million families westward. After the war's conclusion, nearly every state and territory in the West actively courted new inhabitants with pamphlets, handbills and even agents who were sent to northwest Europe to lure people to the promise of America. The burgeoning United States needed hands to work its soil—which would prove fertile in some places and unyielding in others—and to serve in any variety of commercial capacities.

The surge westward was dynamically powered by the railroad lines. They tendered reduced fares to immigrants, and with the wide swaths of land the government had granted the rail companies along their rights-of-way, they offered inexpensive farmlands to potential citizens from England, Germany, Scandinavia, France and elsewhere. The giant railroad concerns needed men to lay the rails, to work them, and to maintain them—and the westerly thrust fomented a burning hunger for artisans and laborers in mills and factories as well. Without newcomers in these fields, the nation's industries could never have become the titans that they did. The country would have been a very different place.

For many who had already made America their home, the sheer number of new faces was alarming, and all too often, rancor was the order of the day. Nevertheless, the unremitting flow of people continued. In 1880 the population of the U.S. was 50 million. Over the next four decades, nearly half that many immigrants would cross our borders. Northwest Europe continued to be an important point of embarkation, but émigrés from other cultures were now vying to take their place in the land of promise. These "new immigrants," as they were called by the old ones, came from all over, with Southern and Eastern Europeans now having the biggest impact. If their reasons for leaving were familiar—economic, mostly, although some fled persecution—it was becoming increasingly easy to coax them into moving. The United States was looking like a successful enterprise, for one thing, and by this time, extended rail lines abroad were able to deliver passengers to ports from which new and improved steamship routes made for safer, swifter passages. It was cheaper, too, to travel, as companies slashed rates in the battle for customer share.

The resistance faced by the Irish, and to a lesser extent the Germans, was that much tougher for these new immigrants, who hailed from Italy, Austria-Hungary, Russia, Bulgaria, Greece, Romania, Turkey and so on. These people looked different, many of them darker, and they spoke in tongues that were entirely incomprehensible. Perhaps most important, they were nearly all Roman Catholics and Jews.

The frigid reception led to a kind of tribalism, wherein the new immigrants stayed in pockets of their own kind, so that, unsurprisingly, there was frequent friction between nationalities. And this in turn retarded the acquisition of their most vital skill—the ability to speak English—or even more likely, made it entirely out of the question.

These latest set foot on these shores, and they then did not venture far from where they landed. The end result is this staggering statistic: Some 98 percent of them made their homes in cities. What it meant to be an American was being redefined. In 1850, 87 percent of the country resided in rural communities. By 1920, more than half of all Americans lived in cities. The fabric of society was being rewoven—its texture, pattern and colors.

The Steerage, by Alfred Stieglitz

Ellis Island lies in New York Harbor. The little bit of land became famous the world over in 1892 when it became the New York–area headquarters for the federal Immigration and Naturalization Service. By the time it closed in 1954, more than 12 million people had used this portal to enter the United States. It has been said that 40 percent of all Americans can trace their roots to someone who passed through here. Above, steerage passengers are jammed onto the decks of the SS *Patricia* as she makes her approach.

Culver Pictures (3)

Ships coming into New York Harbor from overseas were met by inspectors, and most of the first- and second-class passengers were processed and sent along. The great majority of immigrants, however, were poor, and arrived in steerage. All of these had to go to Ellis Island for thorough examinations, as they were often suffering from some ailment or other. They were promptly issued numbers, which they wore in plain view, and men and women were separated.

The screening was rigorous, and any number of physical disorders, even something like cataracts, could very well mean that an alien would immediately be returned to his homeland. Applicants were interrogated closely, and if their answers were unsatisfactory, detention of an hour, or even months, might ensue.

Brown Brothers

Culver Pictures

Underwood Archives

These children look like any other children, except that
here, on Ellis Island, they are playing outside while
their parents are inside, waiting to learn their fate. Their
families are up for deportation, and their appeals are being
considered in Washington, D.C. During its years of service,
Ellis Island was increasingly used less for bringing people
in and more for getting rid of those deemed unsuitable.
In the 1930s it was America's primary deportation center.

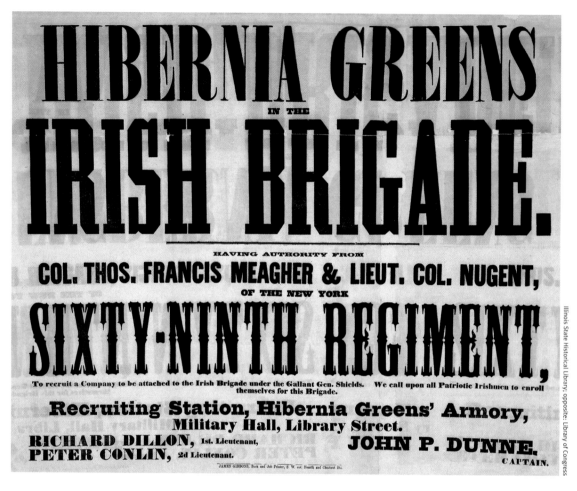

HIBERNIA GREENS
IN THE
IRISH BRIGADE.

HAVING AUTHORITY FROM
COL. THOS. FRANCIS MEAGHER & LIEUT. COL. NUGENT,
OF THE NEW YORK
SIXTY-NINTH REGIMENT,

To recruit a Company to be attached to the Irish Brigade under the Gallant Gen. Shields.   We call upon all Patriotic Irishmen to enroll themselves for this Brigade.

Recruiting Station, Hibernia Greens' Armory,
Military Hall, Library Street.

RICHARD DILLON, 1st. Lieutenant,   **JOHN P. DUNNE,**
PETER CONLIN, 2d Lieutenant.   CAPTAIN.

JAMES GIBBONS, Book and Job Printer, S. W. cor. Fourth and Chestnut Sts.

The Irish-born Thomas Francis Meagher lived a life as fabulous as those in the Celtic legends. An instigator for Irish independence, he was transported by the British to Tasmania but escaped and made his way to New York City. Even as he kept up the drumbeat for Irish nationalism, he was morphing into an American patriot and war hero. With the advent of the Civil War, he joined the Union Army and, after his first hitch, began raising a unit of Irish volunteers that would become the 63rd, 69th and 88th regiments. Meagher's Irish Brigade drew the nastiest assignments— "Bloody Lane" at Antietam, below Marye's Heights at Fredericksburg, in the Wheatfield at Gettysburg—and suffered enormous casualties, while always battling ferociously. "Ah, yes, that Fighting 69th," said Robert E. Lee admiringly, bestowing the famous nickname. After the war, Meagher served as acting governor of Montana. In 1867 he fell off a boat in the Missouri River and drowned. They say he had been drinking. Right: the 69th at Sunday Mass.

PAWNEE
KANSAS TER.

COME ONE · COME ALL!

PUBLIC SALE OF LOTS!!

In consequence of numerous applications from persons desirous of building immediately, the trustees are induced to announce

A SALE OF LOTS

to take place at an earlier date than that already advertised.

There will therefore be TWO Sales of Lots in PAWNEE, one on the 10th of APRIL and the other on the 15th of MAY next.

The situation of PAWNEE is such as scarcely to admit a doubt of its becoming in a short time a large and important place. Being at the head of navigation of the Kansas it is the most delightful starting point for persons emigrating to our more western territories. A Military road from Pawnee to Bridgers Pass in the Rocky Mountains affords the most direct route to Utah, California and Oregon, whilst the road to New Mexico is considerably shortened by a new one recently made. The Military post of Fort Riley is scarcely distant a mile from Pawnee and the government business connected with it will mostly be transacted here.

Ample accomodations will be ready for persons attending the SALES. These as above stated will be on the 10th of April and 15th of May next.

TERMS.--Half the purchase money in cash; the ballance on completion of the title.

W. R. MONTGOMERY,
WILLIAM A. HAMMOND,
R. C. MILLER, } Trustees.
N. LYON,
R. H. HIGGINS.

PAWNEE, K. T., March 12th, 1855. [HERALD OFFICE PRINT, Leavenworth, K. T.]

In the foothills of the Rockies, these pioneers take a breather from their long, arduous trek. The search for an idyllic piece of land was continually drawing people westward.

These homestead photos were all taken in Nebraska. At left, a windmill takes advantage of a power source that is abundant in the prairies, making it possible to pump water from a deep well. Below, a family poses outside their sod house. Opposite: This family doesn't want the folks back East to know they are living in a sod house, but do want to make it clear that they have a splendid organ.

For some people, land wasn't their foremost concern. They wanted money, and the instant riches of a gold rush could be mighty intoxicating. Mining towns like the one seen here sprang up in a heartbeat. Deadwood, S.D., was founded the year this picture was taken, 1876, as 25,000 miners scurried to this outpost in the Black Hills. Gamblers were also drawn to such towns—men like Wild Bill Hickok, who was shot dead here in Deadwood holding aces and eights, on August 2 of this very year. That poker hand will forever be known as the dead man's hand.

Culver Pictures

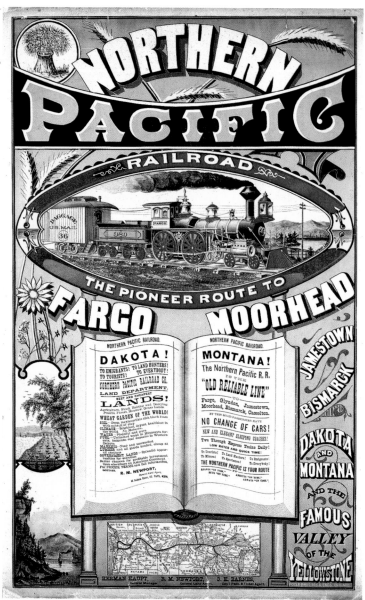

The importance of the railroad to the burgeoning nation, and the role played by immigrants, cannot be overestimated; the newcomers did most of the work. Here, rail workers gather after supper for a portrait. Indian visitors may be seen in the foreground. Left: The rail companies had vast tracts of land to sell at reasonable rates. Bottom left: Union Pacific surveyors on difficult terrain.

Opposite, top: A rail crew building the Northern Pacific link between Minnesota and the Washington Territory pauses at a mountain trestle in 1885. Bottom: Chinese laborers carting dirt in the Sierra Nevada mountains, circa 1877. Above: Celebrating the relationship between the rails and the land, this engine in Atchison, Kan., in 1880 is bedecked with icons extolling the bounty of the fertile local soil.

He was a poor Irish farmer. She was a dreamer who heard about free land in a place called Oklahoma. They fled to America and joined the Oklahoma Land Rush, one of the wildest giveaways in history. They were Tom Cruise and Nicole Kidman in the 1992 film *Far and Away*, but the Land Rush was real. After the Dawes Act of 1887 cut Indian holdings, the government said that 160-acre parcels in the Oklahoma Territory would be awarded to the swiftest. At noon on April 22, 1889, thousands poured across the border to instantly settle the last major unsettled area in the U.S. Ever since, Oklahomans have been called Sooners, after those who jumped the gun in their lust for land.

This was life on the mean streets of New York City. Jacob Riis took the photo above of an alley called Bandits' Roost. His images of slum conditions shocked the general public. Opposite: the hurly-burly of the Lower East Side. Left: Perched on a milk can outside his tenement, a boy ponders the world.

Lewis W. Hine took these photographs in New York City during the years 1908–1915. Members of the Malatesta family, including four-year-old Lizzie, fashion artificial flowers in their home. They are paid six cents a gross. Below, women sort through old rags in a textile factory. Opposite: A girl brings work home from her factory job.

Within one horrific half hour, 146 workers perished, nearly all of them immigrant seamstresses, some as young as 13. When flames broke out at the Triangle Shirtwaist Company on the eighth floor of the "fireproof" Asch Building in New York City on March 25, 1911, the workers tried desperately to flee—but the owners had locked the doors to keep employees at their stations. That left only one fire escape (below), which collapsed under their feet. Many jumped to their deaths. When it was over, public outcry led to laws that would protect laborers.

In a rare moment of repose, a Hungarian steelworker in Pittsburgh plays his accordion. This 1908 photograph was taken by Lewis Hine.

This portrait of a Czech grandmother is a classic example of Hine's ability to capture the many faces of the immigrant.

Despite her burden, this Italian immigrant strides the city streets with fortitude in 1910.

A grocer displays his wares—vegetables, eggs and spices—in San Francisco's Chinatown.

Japanese women disembark at the newly opened Angel Island Immigration Station in 1910. For many Asians, America held the promise of a place where work would surely lead to fortune. But the "Ellis Island of the West" functioned mainly to keep them out. Known by officials as the "Guardian of the Western Gate," the beautiful but isolated isle in the San Francisco Bay quickly became a detention center. There, for months or even years, mostly Chinese hopefuls (the Japanese would later become yoked with them as a "yellow peril" that worried American workers) waited to know their fate— immigration or deportation? Cut off from the outside world, they endured humiliating medical exams and interrogations. Many Chinese expressed their loneliness and frustration by carving poems into the barracks walls. One detainee had clearly lost his golden dream of America: "Even if it is built of jade, it has turned into a cage."

Lewis Hine traveled the nation to document the travails of children who were coming of age on the job rather than in the classroom. Without schooling, their upside potential was limited, to say the least. Images like these were instrumental in the enactment of laws banning child labor. At left, circa 1911, these "breaker boys" in South Pittston, Pa., separated coal from slate. The West Virginia boy above, in 1908, has been working long shifts as a driver in a coal mine every day for a year.

As Hine's images heartbreakingly reveal, the little workers of the immigrant class were surely fair game for other than the coal mines. Clockwise from above: In 1908 a girl works the line at a South Carolina cotton mill; in 1912 barefoot kids pick cotton in Texas; five-year-old Salvin lugs two pecks of cranberries in New Jersey in 1910.

After Henry Ford ignited the auto boom with his Model T in 1908, Detroit became a mecca for job-seekers the world over. Ford's River Rouge plant would employ more than 100,000, and they included Poles, Germans, Mexicans, and Arabs from Syria and Lebanon. Ford sought to turn them all into the same thing: solid citizens and hard workers. The first phrase they learned at the company's English school was "I am a good American." Upon graduating, they participated in an onstage ceremony in which, dressed in the native garb of their homeland, they walked into a huge "melting pot," then emerged in good ol' American clothes. Henry Ford was seen by some as a benevolent father to his workers, by others as a zealot who stripped men of their cultural identity.

Ford (below and opposite) was a descendant of Irish immigrants who made the journey on coffin ships. He appreciated the value of a warm bed, a tidy room and lace curtains—and he instructed his workers, including these Russian immigrants, of their worth. Ford's wealth and influence were evidence of the rising immigrant classes.

All-American Music

The Beatles said they were nothing without Elvis; Eric Clapton is a disciple of American blues. Ireland's Chieftains seek to honor country music by recording with Emmylou Harris. But all this homage is a bit off the beat.

The way to think about American music is close to the way we think about America, a land of opportunity, diversity and—as important—assimilation and invention. The slaves from Africa bequeathed the blues, a lamentation with basic rhythms that underlies rock 'n' roll, rap and whatever tomorrow brings. Scottish and Irish folk songs led not only to Woody Guthrie and Bob Dylan, but also to Willie Nelson, Faith Hill and even Kid Rock.

If there is a Model T of American music—a greatest invention among several—it is jazz. In New Orleans in the late 19th century, African and island rhythms blended with gospel and Cajun, and—bam!—out popped Louis Armstrong. The blues informed a white man named Jimmie Rodgers and the hill folk known as the Carter Family, who brought Scots-based singing to the mix and created

American folk as well as country. In the 20th century, the pot bubbled over as Jewish immigrants and second-generation Americans scripted Tin Pan Alley tunes and, finally, the Great American Songbook. George Gershwin, Richard Rodgers, Jerome Kern and particularly Irving Berlin added nationalism to klezmer and a host of other European influences to create "standards," which were rendered immortally by the children or grandchildren of immigrants, such singers as Bing Crosby, Frank Sinatra and Fred Austerlitz (to you, Astaire). There were other, female singers who knew the blues but could sing it all: Bessie Smith, Billie Holiday. Today, few have settled on just what Norah Jones is. This daughter of Indian sitarist Ravi Shankar and Texan Sue Jones has her way with jazz, pop, country—and yet seems uniquely herself.

Even classical music has taken on American shadings. Take Leonard Bernstein. His eclectic compositions, for both the concert hall and the Broadway stage, hearken to heaven and to the New York City streets—and most places in between.

One of jazz's first stars, Joe "King" Oliver (opposite, far left), led a band that included a young trumpeter named Louis Armstrong (center). Left: Leonard Bernstein, born in 1918 to middle-class Jewish immigrants in Massachusetts, was a composer and conductor of genius, as well as a deft democratizer of classical music. His young-people's concerts on TV drew new generations to Beethoven, Brahms, Mozart. Below: In Virginia, the Carter clan (seen here in 1941) made music that combined Celtic influences with exotic touches such as the banjo, which was of African origin.

Gjon Mili

Charles Trainor

Sid Avery/MPTV

Billie Holiday's grandfather was the child of a black Virginia slave and a white Irish plantation owner; her mother was 13 when Billie was born. Elvis was what Memphis record producer Sam Phillips had been waiting for: a white singer who sounded black. Frank Sinatra, of Hoboken, N.J., the son of Italian immigrants, worked hard to rid his delivery of any Joisey accent.

Cornell Capa

Jerome Kern said of the man at left, "Irving Berlin has no place in American music. He *is* American music." That's quite an assessment of one who was born Israel Baline in Russia in 1888. Berlin wrote "White Christmas," and was George M. Cohan's equal in patriotic song ("God Bless America" is his). Below: Norah Jones, a poster girl for multiculturalism, is signed to a jazz label, for which she interprets Hank Williams, among others.

Clay Patrick McBride/Retna Ltd.

Playing by the Numbers

1921–1964

Still they would come, the hopeful yearners, and once again the vast playing field was ashift. This was a different world, after the Great War, and certainly no less so for those with an eye on America. And even as they gazed, they saw the rules changing.

There had been, earlier, a few "refinements" in immigration and naturalization laws. The first substantive legislation was the Chinese Exclusion Act of 1882, which banned Chinese laborers from entering the country for 10 years (the measure was subsequently extended). Thus was ended centuries of unfettered immigration. In 1891, polygamists were deemed ineligible, as were "persons suffering from a loathsome or a dangerous contagious disease" and anyone convicted of "a misdemeanor involving moral turpitude."

In 1917 it was decreed that adults had to be able to read and write to gain admission. This was supposed to assuage widespread fears that "the wrong sort" of people were getting in, "less desirable breeds" who were also grabbing up jobs that might otherwise have gone to "real" Americans. In just a few years, though, the literacy requirement was no longer having its desired effect: Southern and Eastern Europeans were preparing themselves for the test.

Once more there arose ardent clamoring for change. Congress responded in 1921 with the Emergency Quota Act, whereby restrictions were placed on newcomers from Europe, the Near East, Africa and Australia. It was the first time a limit was set on the number of U.S. immigrants allowed: 357,803 annually. Further, the law stated that each nationality was limited to 3 percent of the foreign-born populace that was resident in 1910, meaning that the "old immigrant" countries in northwest Europe would be favored over the "new immigrant" lands in Southern and Eastern Europe.

This quota system was initially intended as a stopgap measure but in fact turned out to be the guiding principle in U.S. immigration policies until 1965. The Immigration Act of 1924 merely expanded on this "national origins" basis—and bias. Known as the Johnson-Reed Act, it slashed the non–Western Hemisphere quota to 164,667, of which four fifths was allotted to northwestern Europe. For example, the precise quota for Germans was 51,227, while for Italians it was 3,845. As another example, exactly 124 Armenians could come forward as potential citizens.

So, immigration figures plummeted from pre-WWI levels, and this decline was abetted by the nasty appearance of the Great Depression in 1929. From 1931 to 1940, a mere half million people moved to America. The relative paucity of this number is perhaps better appreciated when you know that more people left the country than came in during those years.

While the numbers were low, one unusual and very important development was afoot. Primarily because of Hitler's rise to power in Germany, many Jews there and in neighboring lands sought refuge, and in consequence some two dozen Nobel laureates made their way to the United States. These included Albert Einstein from Germany, the preeminent scientist of the 20th century, and Italy's Enrico Fermi, who became one of the chief architects of the Atomic Age.

During WWII, China was allied with the U.S., and the ban on immigrants from there was lifted. However, another group with Asian roots was treated less well. With America wrapped in the frightening embrace of all-out war, residents of Japanese descent—even those who were U.S. citizens—were placed in spartan detainee camps for the duration of the conflict. Ironically, the absence of Japanese Americans opened the door for Mexican day laborers to enter the country legally in order to fill the need for manual workers. This *bracero* program provided an income, albeit small, for 200,000 Mexicans during WWII and represented an important stage in Latin American migration to the United States.

There was another intriguing, and unforeseen, result from the war. With so many men serving overseas, a great many cross-cultural romances were kindled, and some of these led to the altar. Quite a few actually, as the War Brides Act of 1945 permitted more than a hundred thousand American soldiers to bring back wives, and sometimes children, from far-flung lands.

For so many others, the war had much less happy consequences. There were some 50 million people on the move after its end, many known as displaced persons, or DPs. These poor souls had for various reasons been uprooted by the violence and had nowhere to go. In 1948 a policy was adopted that allowed 205,000 refugees to enter the U.S. over a two-year span. Later, that number nearly doubled.

In 1952, immigration laws were revised yet again to make it easier for skilled workers, for parents of American citizens and for the immediate families of permanent resident aliens to enter the country. However, the national-origins quota system was, if anything, tightened, and "internal security" measures were toughened. President Harry S Truman was displeased with the most stringent legislation, but it would remain American policy for another decade.

It is September 1944 and World War II is still ablaze, but for this Scottish bride and her American groom, all is well.

Sam Goldwyn (opposite, in 1942) began every day with a two-to-five-mile walk. The Polish immigrant was forced out of what would become MGM, but he enjoyed a long string of commercial and financial successes. His motto: Pictures are for entertainment; messages should be delivered by Western Union.

Culver Pictures

Jewish immigrants from Eastern Europe found it tough to crack the American business scene, so a few of them went west and essentially built an industry of their own—Hollywood. Above: Russian-born Louis B. Mayer came to the U.S. in 1907. Here, he exudes the kind of intensity that let him rule over Metro-Goldwyn-Mayer from 1924 to 1951. His films were often morality plays in which good conquers evil; that is to say, real Americans are decent people who do the right thing. Jack Warner (right, arriving at the Oscars in 1963) was the youngest of a dozen children born to Polish immigrants. For decades he was the production chief at Warner Bros., whose movies became known in the '30s for, among other things, a gritty, realistic portrayal of immigrants forced into a world of violent crime.

Julian Wasser

Actors from all over heard the siren call of Hollywood. For the silent movies, if they didn't speak English—well, that was O.K., as long as they looked good and could maybe emote a bit. Above: Greta Garbo and director Mauritz Stiller arrive from Sweden in 1925. She was mega; he wasn't. Left: Rudolph Valentino's smoky Italian allure hypnotized fans. Right: Bob Hope was born in England, so he had no problem with the lingo. That's him on the left in 1908 at age five, with brothers Fred, Jack and Sid.

As war with fascism wreaked havoc in their homelands, many artists left for the U.S. Above: Leading German architect Ludwig Mies van der Rohe (left), who became a citizen in 1944, confers with a student at the Illinois Institute of Technology. Mies van der Rohe dreamed of glass skyscrapers—and he built them, forever altering America's cityscapes. Russian émigré Vladimir Nabokov (right), a citizen since 1945, enjoyed writing in his car, as here in 1958. For his novel *Lolita,* he filled 94 index cards with manuscript notes. Some dismissed the work as pornography; *Vanity Fair* called it "the only convincing love story of our century." Opposite: George Szell, one of the greatest conductors of the 20th century, leads the Cleveland Orchestra at New York City's Carnegie Hall. Born in Budapest, Szell settled in the U.S. in 1939, and won his citizenship in 1946.

Hansel Mieth

Hulton-Deutsch Collection/Corbis

On December 7, 1941, the Japanese Empire blasted Pearl Harbor in a terrifying surprise attack that pulled America into World War II. Answering to a fearful and suspicious public, the U.S. government "relocated" some 120,000 West Coast Japanese Americans (men, women and children; it did not matter that they might be citizens) to internment camps, where most would remain until war's end. At left, an American soldier keeps guard at California's Manzanar camp, the first to open. Above, American soldiers of Japanese descent visit with their families and friends in the Heart Mountain camp in Wyoming.

Above, a Marine is thrilled by the sight of his British war bride and their son in 1946. At right, that same year, Sgt. Donald Holdaway and his bride from India embrace. They had met in Calcutta, where she was working for the U.S. Army Air Forces. Left: In December 1948, the new citizens were still arriving en masse. Here, a plane from Hamburg brings to America German war brides, children and fiancées.

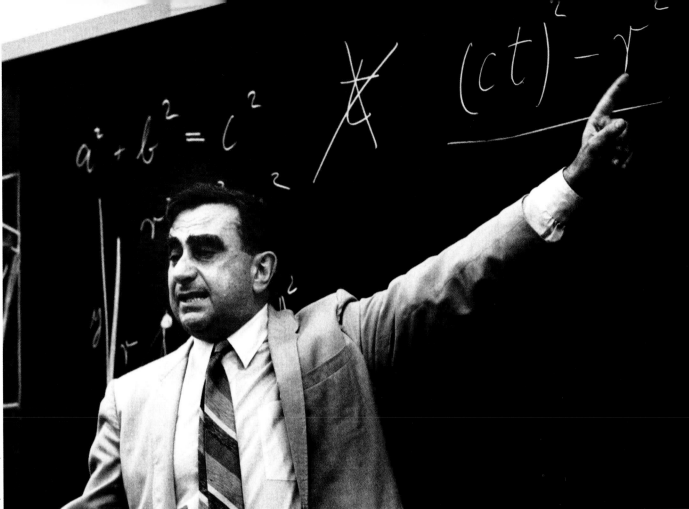

The World War II era brought many leading scientists to America. Opposite: Enrico Fermi came to the U.S. from Italy in 1938. Working in Chicago in 1942, he directed tests that led to the first controlled nuclear chain reaction. Above: Hungarian Edward Teller played a key role in U.S. defense strategy, from the A-bomb to Star Wars. Wernher von Braun came from Germany after the war, and helped spur America in the Space Race.

Brown Brothers; opposite: Philippe Halsman

Having renounced his German citizenship when Hitler seized power, Albert Einstein takes the U.S. oath in 1940, along with his daughter, Margot (right), and his secretary, Helen Dukas. As a scientist, Einstein changed our understanding of the universe; as a pacifist, he spoke for understanding among men. America proved an ideal haven for him. Einstein once wrote, "Everything that is really great and inspiring is created by the individual who can labor in freedom." Today, his name is synonymous with genius.

All-American Fun & Games

On the playing fields of Eton, never mind those of Rugby School, they don't want to hear about "American football," a term that seems to them an oxymoron. Further, the soccer fans of China will tell you that the whole ball-kicking enterprise dates back perhaps 2,300 years to the Han Dynasty. And baseball a "national pastime"? Again the English would quarrel, pointing out—not incorrectly—that the stateside innovators of the mid-1800s were more than informally acquainted with the cousin sports cricket and rounders.

But Dr. Naismith did tack peach baskets to 10-foot-high railings in Springfield, Mass., in 1891 to invent the American-as-apple-pie game of basketball, right? Well, yes . . . but he was Canadian-born, and recalled enjoying as a boy a game called duck-on-a-rock, which inspired his thinking on basketball.

America makes no claim on such as golf (Scotland? the Dutch game *kolven*? the French *jeu de mal*?) or tennis (the ancient Egyptians? or the royals of 11th century France?). And we admit that chess and checkers might have come from ancient Ur, undergoing refinement in European variations.

So, is there no game that we can call our own?

Well, there's one solid candidate. The French-sounding lacrosse originated with Native Americans. In its original version, it was a brutal sport—the "Little Brother of War"—used to train tribes for combat. Goals could be miles apart, and lacrosse sticks were used in weapon-like fashion by hundreds of "players" at a time.

And that name? French settlers, having seen the natives compete, noted the shape of the curved stick, *la croix.* Montrealers of the mid-19th century were probably the first white North Americans to play lacrosse, and today the sport is called by some Canada's Game—just as Americans call baseball their national pastime.

Brown Brothers

Wayne Miller/Magnum

Underwood & Underwood/Corbis

Opposite: In San Francisco's Chinatown, a boy prepares to snap the football. Above: In two settings, one pastoral and one in the south side of Chicago, these other lads prepare to take their mighty swipes at the baseball. Left: action at the 1926 Ladies Lacrosse League of America's championships.

In 1948, kids play chess. In '49, an Amish lass, Emma Miller, wins the girls' national marbles tournament in Asbury Park, N.J. Marbles, too, has ancient ancestors, deriving from a Roman game called nuts. Various claims are made for the origins of hopscotch; one holds that it was a British training exercise for eluding mines in World War I.

Nina Leen

George Silk

Ralph Morse

Brown Brothers

Golf made its way
across the pond in
the latter half of the
19th century, and in
1890 is essayed by
these women of
Wellesley College,
near Boston. One
hundred years later,
a man and girl take
a turn on a seesaw in
Bridgehampton, N.Y.

Elliott Erwitt/Magnum

Our Diverse Nation

1965–Present

A small craft teeming with a cargo of fragile dreams makes for America from the hardscrabble shores of Haiti in 1981. Many such refugees were returned to Haiti. Others were permitted to enter. Still others entered without permission.

The mid-1960s heralded immense social upheaval in the United States, and, appropriately, the Immigration Act of 1965 proved to be an important factor in the "new" society. The redrawn rules and numbers may not seem all that significant on the surface: Overall quotas would be based on hemispheres rather than national origin, 170,000 people from the Eastern and 120,000 from the Western. But what this meant was, the inherently racist "nativism" would no longer determine who would be among the new arrivals. Further, in an effort to reunite separated families, the spouses, parents and children of American citizens would not be factored into the quota system at all. In short, the Third World was about to become part of America's world.

In the years following, there came a handful of other laws that for the most part opened our doors even wider to those who wished to enter—and entering were a few from Europe but many more from Mexico and the Philippines, Vietnam and the Dominican Republic, India, Pakistan, Korea, Puerto Rico, even Cuba. This was, in the broadest sense, a melting pot of stunningly diverse flavors and textures.

If it was a new kind of immigration, there were aspects of the process that seemed, even in the modern age, immutable. For the most part, the vast differences represented in the multicultural mix did not quickly blend or soften, but tended to linger in a pluralistic fashion as the Haitians lived with the Haitians, and the Indians with the Indians. Within major urban centers, enclaves known as Little Italy faded when third-generation climbers headed for the 'burbs, other neighborhoods suddenly sprouting up, such as Little Havana or Little India. Just as with immigrants of old, the newest newcomers were most at ease with their own accents, and foods, and hobbies. And just as with their predecessors, many of them often had no alternative but to hang with the family. Even in a society that enjoyed unprecedented mobility—both literally and figuratively—economic facts of life (and sometimes bias) forced many new Americans to go slowly. Baby steps were taken with trepidation. Yes, these immigrants had a vastly improved chance to assimilate more quickly than those of yore, but America was a big and daunting place, and the pattern generally prevailed: Settle in before setting out.

The liberalization that took place in the 1960s has been followed by periods of cheering the new America—where the most recent additions to the citizenry have sparked great gains in technology, industry and invention—but also shouting for the borders to be closed. Fear of foreigners has escalated in the post-9/11 period, and the debate over immigration policy now informs national and many local elections.

This, of course, does nothing to diminish America's stature as The Dream to those looking in from outside. They still want—need—to try America, taste America, drink of America. And so, 19 suffocate in an overheated truck coming in from Mexico; 134 who have paid smugglers thousands to deliver them to the land of the free are sent back to China when their overburdened ship runs aground in New York; hundreds try each year to make the midnight run from Cuba or Haiti in a speedboat or on a raft. Illegal immigration is seen by many as a scourge. But in the act, nothing is so dramatic and alternately inspiring or tragic, nothing is as illustrative of the allure of America and the success of America, as people risking all to become Americans.

And if they succeed, as with so many who have come before, there will be trials, gauntlets even. The ones who have come before will always cling to their precious toehold, their hard-earned gains. For the most recent arrivals, the newest of the new, the future will contain days of doubt, and even remorse . . .

At least at home everyone spoke the same language. I knew where I stood.

But then, perhaps they will recall that the situation they left behind was dismal, nowhere really, and there wasn't any possibility of anything getting any better, no hope even for the children. And then, maybe, this newest immigrant, though he is tired beyond words, will turn anew to the task at hand, somehow reach inside for some strength that will enable him to pound the pavement one more time, to at last find that job, not a great one, heaven knows, but a job . . .

There wasn't work before, where I came from, there wasn't any hope. Now I am permitted hope, hope that if I work hard, we can eat well, maybe even save something. I feel like I have some kind of a chance.

After all, that's why I came here.

At a July 4, 2000, ceremony in Seattle, Alyse MeiLan Campbell, a Chinese girl who had been adopted by Americans, is sworn in as a citizen of the United States.

When the Vietnam War ended in 1975, desperate South Vietnamese scrambled to get out of the country. Many drifted into the South China Sea on fishing boats and rafts. Perhaps half died, but thousands survived starvation, pirates and storms to eventually reach America. Most settled in California or on Texas's Gulf Coast, where they have drawn on their age-old maritime skills to thrive in the shrimping industry. Below, one of the "boat people" boards the USS *White Plains,* clutching all he owns between his teeth. At left, Mai Ly Wong (with her son in San Francisco in 1995) was one of 2,000 babies flown here for adoption in 1975's Operation Babylift.

The Hispanic population in the U.S. has skyrocketed in recent years, to the extent that Latinos have passed African Americans as the country's largest minority. Given their high birth rate, it is estimated that in two generations they will hold one out of every four jobs. Left: Manny Ramirez, the stellar slugger for the Boston Red Sox, is a native of the Dominican Republic. Here, in 2004, he celebrates becoming a citizen. Hispanic players have become a dominant force in the national pastime. Right: The path for illegal immigrants from Mexico has for years been treacherous.

Muslims have increasingly been making their way to our shores. For example, in 1990 they accounted for a 10th of 1 percent of all immigrants to the U.S. By the end of the decade, Muslims—from scores of different countries— made up nearly 45 percent of all newcomers. Here, Tufaha Baydayn, who fled civil war in her native Lebanon in 1982, tends to her lovely front yard in Dearborn, Mich., 20 years later.

Alexandra Avakian/Contact Press

Ours is a country that once imported Africans as slaves. Today, Africans come seeking opportunity. In New York City, the African-born population has quadrupled since 1980. Many are highly educated professionals, the brightest minds and best talents from lands that have been ravaged by poverty and political corruption. Left: 14-year-old soccer prodigy Freddy Adu immigrated from Ghana with his family in 1997, years before anyone knew about his phenomenal feet. His family had won a visa "lottery," a program meant to provide for a more diverse group of American immigrants. In 2003, Freddy became a citizen—and the youngest player in modern American history to be signed to a professional sports team (D.C. United). Above: Many African women have become entrepreneurs here. Fatou Sall, who immigrated from Senegal, displays African clothing and fabrics at her Harlem boutique in 2002.

America has been a perfect fit for these talented immigrants. Left: Romanian gymnast Nadia Comaneci and hubby Bart Conner show off their stuff in Oklahoma in 1996. Below: Of Chinese descent, cellist Yo-Yo Ma (here in 1986) was born in Paris. Opposite: David Ho was born in Taiwan and came to America with his parents. His AIDS research made him *Time*'s Man of the Year in 1996.

Thomas Hoepker/Magnum

Ray Fisher

Just One More

No country has had more immigration stories than the United States of America—literally millions upon millions of them. One of the most recent is as fascinating and unlikely—bizarre, even—as any. Born in Austria in 1947, he was 21 and barely able to speak English when he arrived on these shores. He gained fame as Mr. Universe, a bodybuilding champion, then became a citizen in 1983. He morphed into a movie star, and did his best work portraying barbarians and aliens. In 2003, at age 56, he became the 38th governor of California, the nation's largest state. He is Conan. He is The Terminator. He is Arnold Schwarzenegger.

David Hume Kennerly